How to Use
Children's Pew Activities

This book of reproducible Bible-based *Children's Pew Activities* has been created especially for children who attend church or Sunday school.

Using the Reproducible Pages

Each of the activities in this book appears on two pages. They have been designed to be reproduced on both sides of a piece of paper. The pages can then be folded in half in order to make a booklet for each child. The 15 children's pew activities in this book can be used again and again in your church or Sunday school.

Educational and Fun

Featured on each activity is a Bible story from the Old or New Testament and a memory verse from the Bible for children to learn. Activities are also included and are lots of fun for young children to do. Some of the activities are tracing, coloring, dot-to-dots, and mazes. Because the activities are simple, they require very little supervision to complete.

In-Church Activities

Because the activities presented in this book require only a pencil and crayons to complete, they are perfect for use as in-church activities for children who accompany their parents to services. With very little direction, children will find the activities entertaining and informative.

Sunday School Activities

Make a copy of an activity for each child and use the activities as supplements to regular Sunday school lessons. The activities are perfect for times when additional exercises are needed after the lesson plan is completed. Substitute teachers who need a last minute activity will also find them useful and educational. Teachers can familiarize themselves with each Bible story presented by referring to the citation in the memory verse located at the bottom of each one. They can then read or retell the Bible story to the children and teach them to recite the memory verse.

Take-Home Activities

Children's Pew Activities can be used as Sunday school take-home activities. They are a perfect way for parents to share Bible stories with their children. Children can be encouraged to learn the Bible memory verse on the front of each activity. They can be given an opportunity on the following Sunday to recite the verse in Sunday school. Teachers can keep a simple chart to record the verses recited by each child. The reproducible award on the following page can be awarded to students who learn the verses.

Blessings

to

____
name

who has learned _________ Bible verses.
number

"God is with you in everything you do."
Genesis 21:22

____
signature

GP-75501 Children's Pew Activities

Connect the dots. Color the picture of Noah's ark.

GP-75501 Children's Pew Activities

Color the picture.

The rainbow is a sign of God's promise.

Finish the picture and the word.
Trace the lines.

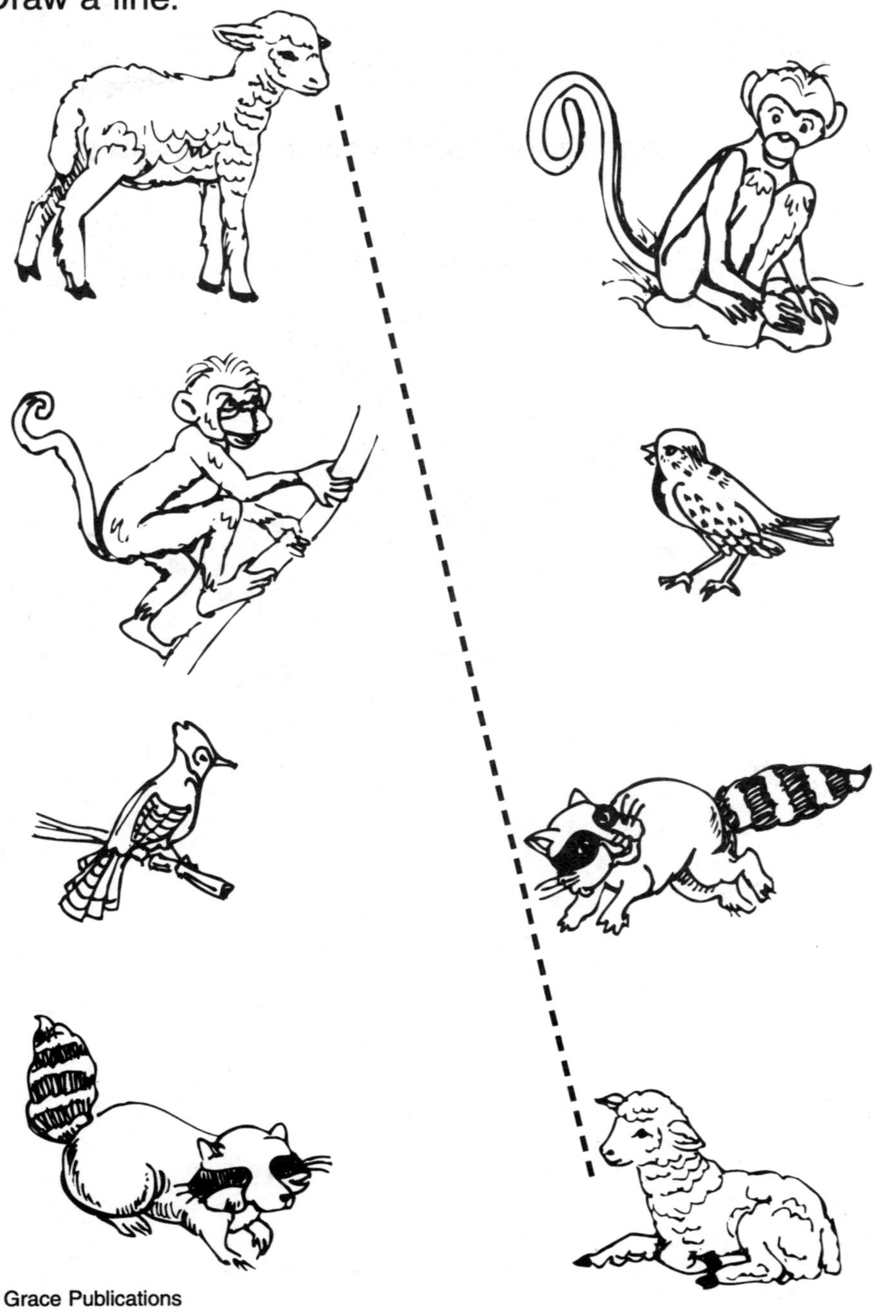

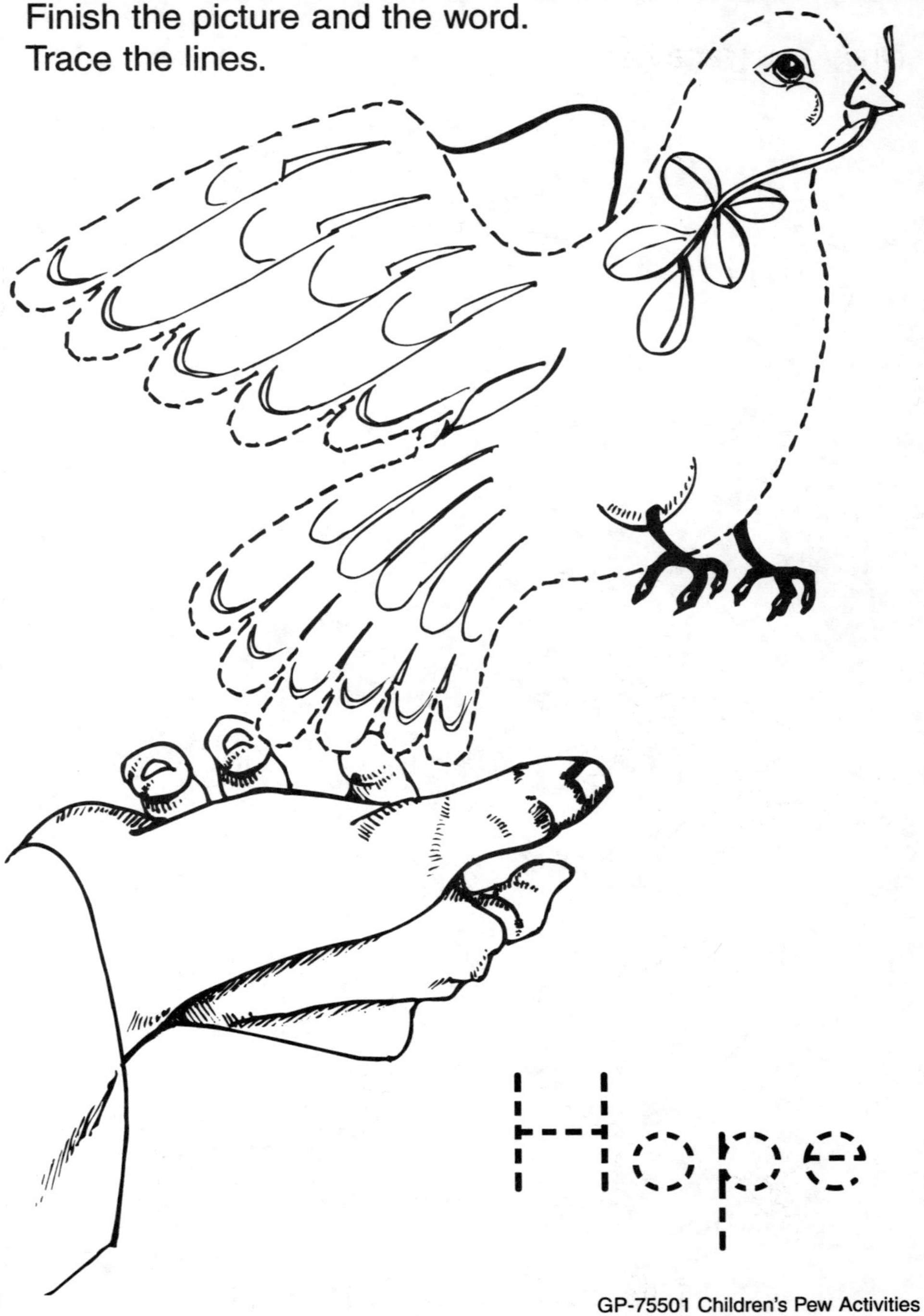

Hope

Draw your face here.

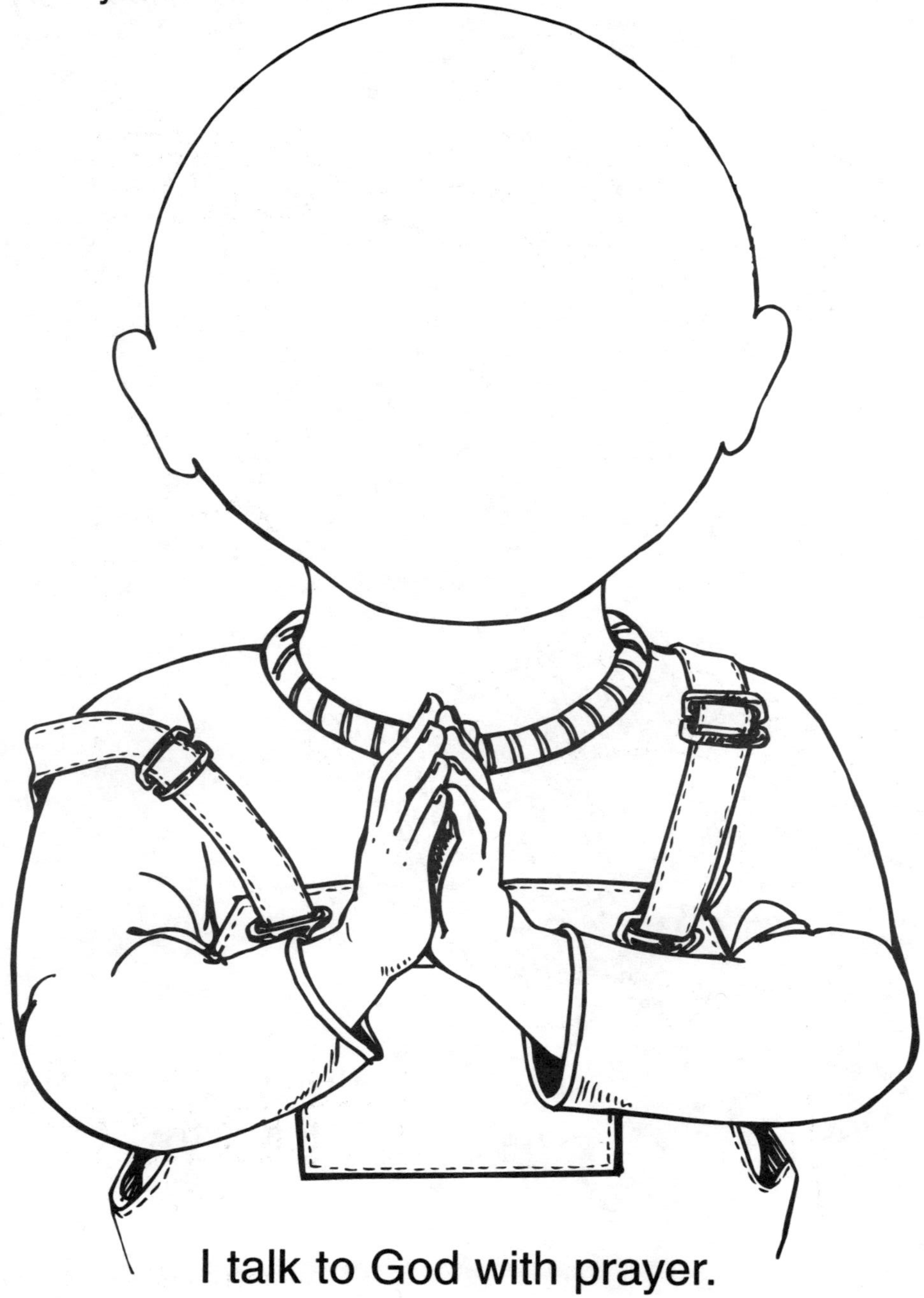

I talk to God with prayer.

Jacob's Ladder

Color the shining ladder Jacob saw in his dream.

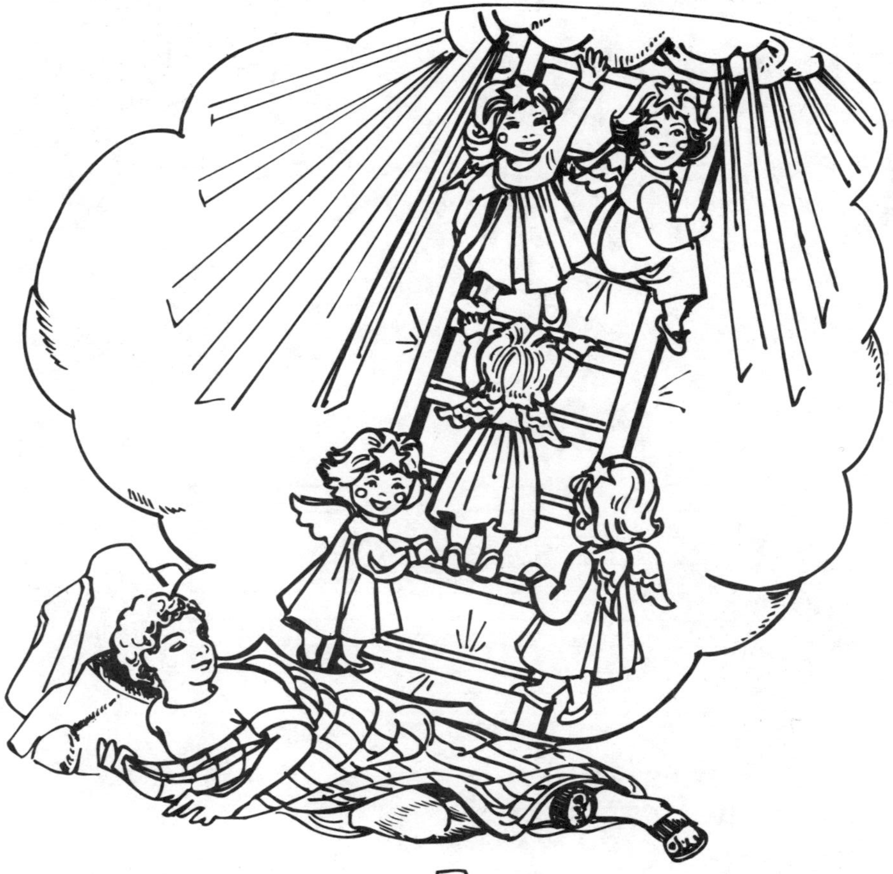

"I am with you and will watch over you wherever you go . . ."
Genesis 28:15

Jacob promised to give God one tenth.
Draw coins in the bank.

We give back to God.

Trace the letters.

Prayer brings us
closer to God.

Joseph and His Brothers

Find the words from Joseph's story.
Circle them in the puzzle.

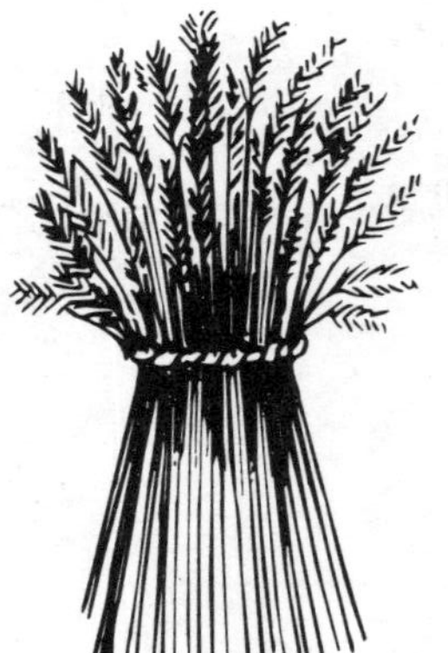

BROTHERS

SLAVE

EGYPT

FORGIVE

ELEVEN

JACOB

JOSEPH

PHARAOH

```
B R O T H E R S A R N
F S L A V E P A X N D
S R O L E L E V E N L
R J P H A R A O H P E
J O S E P H Q K L O C
B H I N D J A C O B X
M U S F O R G I V E P
A Y H C O N E G Y P T
```

Color Joseph's coat with many beautiful colors.

"So then, it was not you who sent me here, but God."
Genesis 45:8

Joseph's Dream

Trace the numbers.
Write the biggest number
in the box.

Joseph had ☐ brothers.

Write the correct letter in each space.

 = O    = A

 = E   ♥ = I

J ___ S ___ P H

F ___ R G ___ V ___

H ___ S

♥

B R ___ T H ___ R S.

God gave Moses the words to say to help his people.
Trace the lines.

God's Word

Moses and the Bulrushes

Connect the dots.
Color the picture of baby Moses.

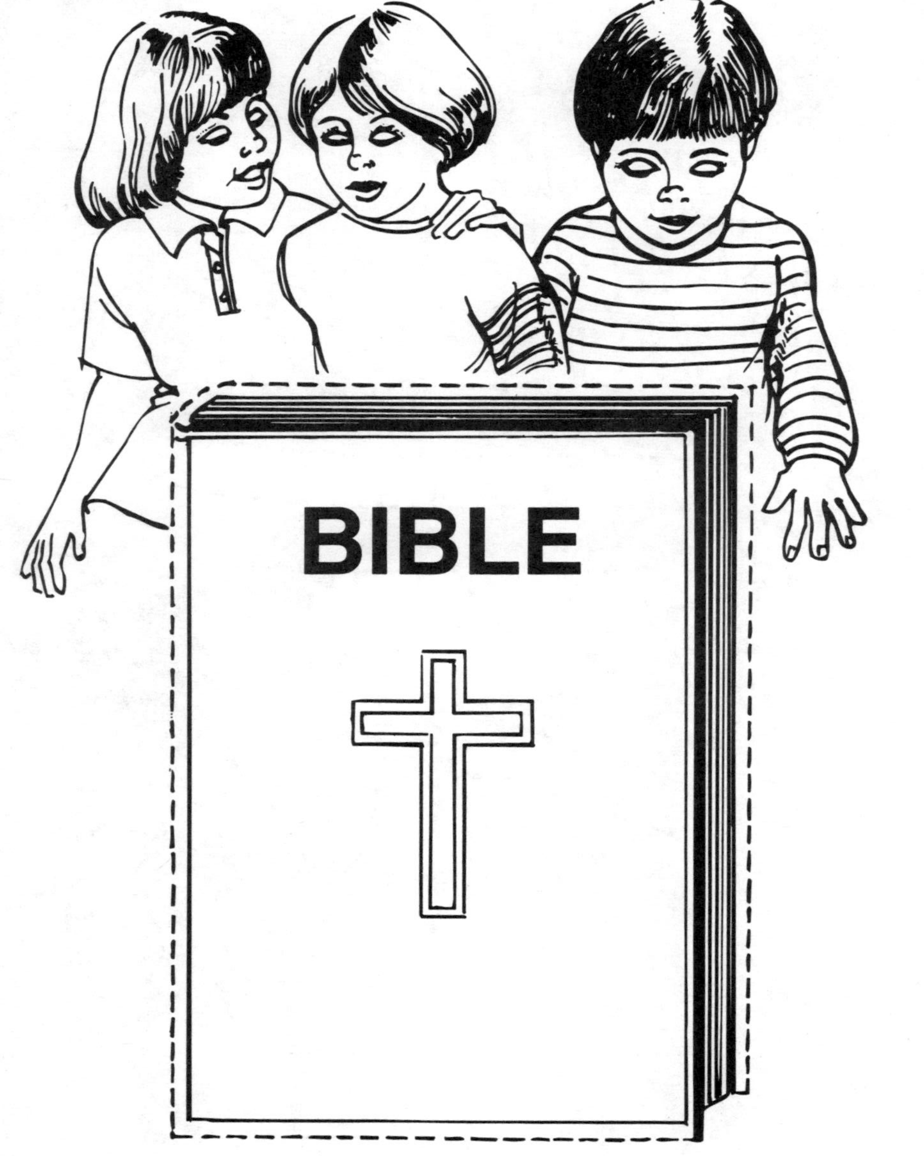

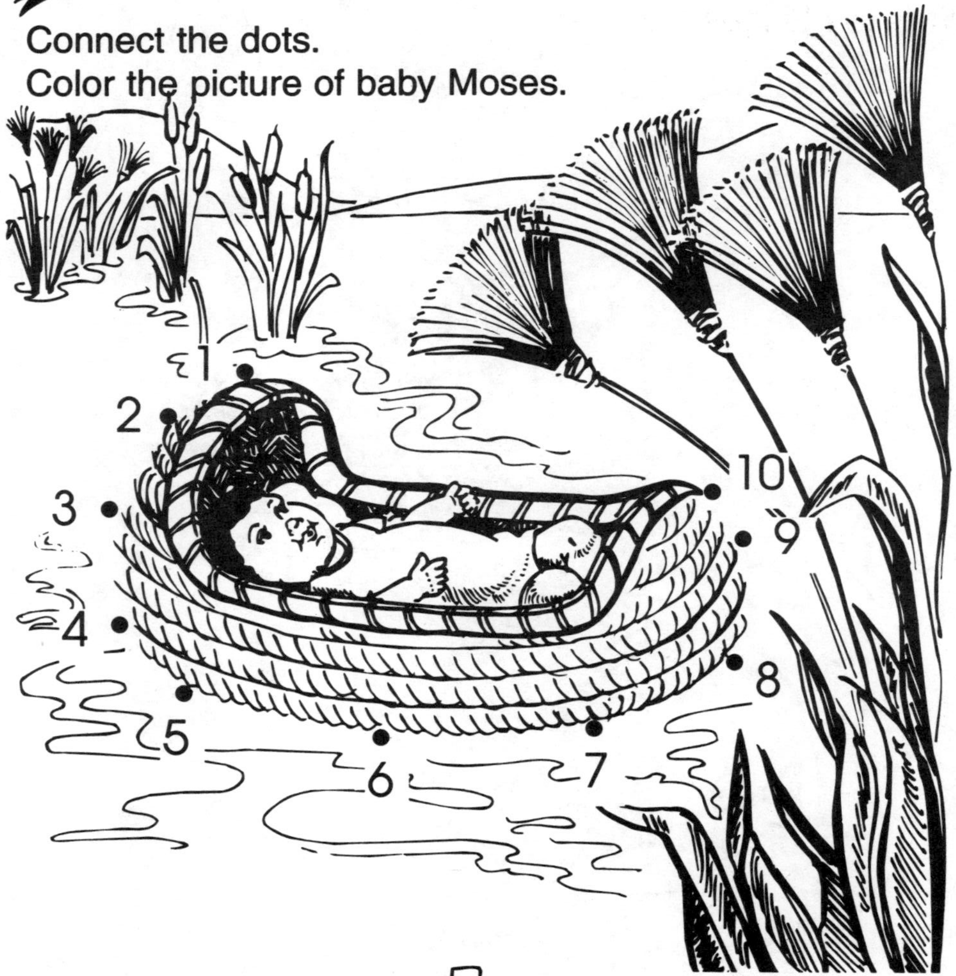

And God said, "I will be with you."
Exodus 3:12

God spoke to Moses
from the burning bush.
Trace the words of God.

"I AM WHO I AM."

God sent Moses and Aaron to tell Pharaoh,
"Let my people go!"
Color the path.

Moses

Color some ways to be still.

Moses and the Ten Commandments

Color the picture of Moses and the stone tablets.

"The Lord is my strength and my song;
he has become my salvation."
Exodus 15:2

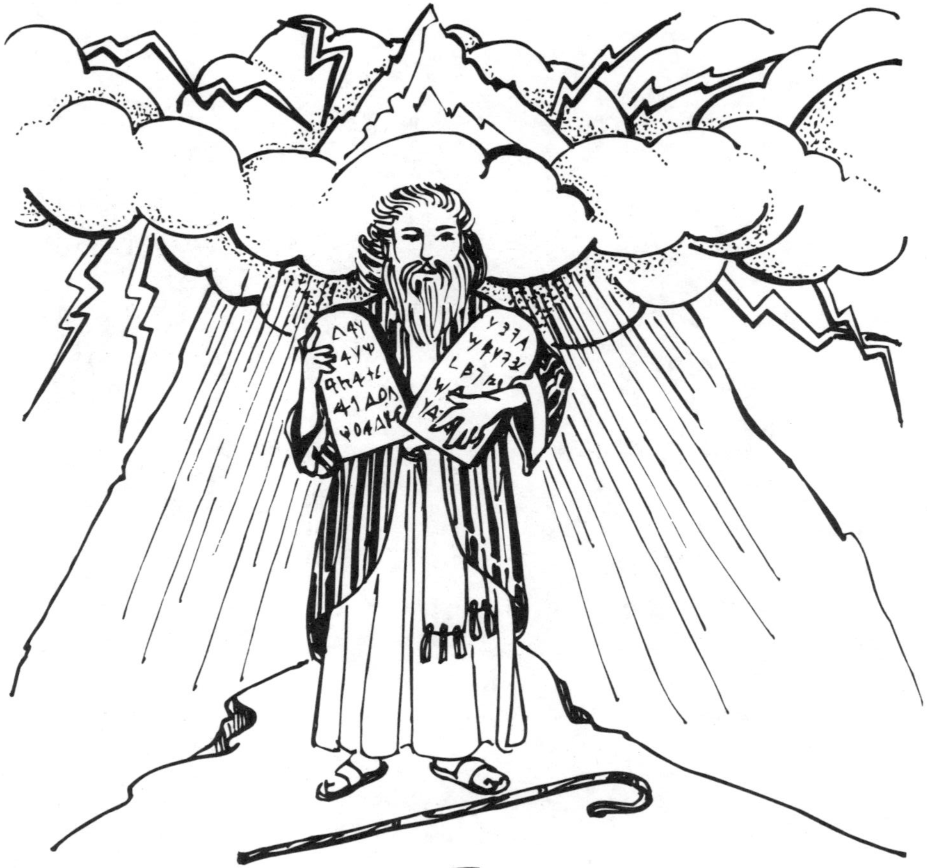

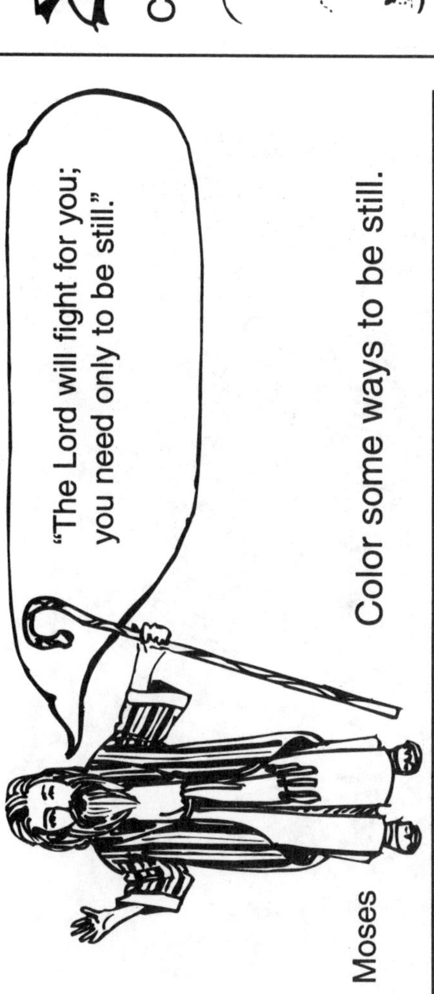

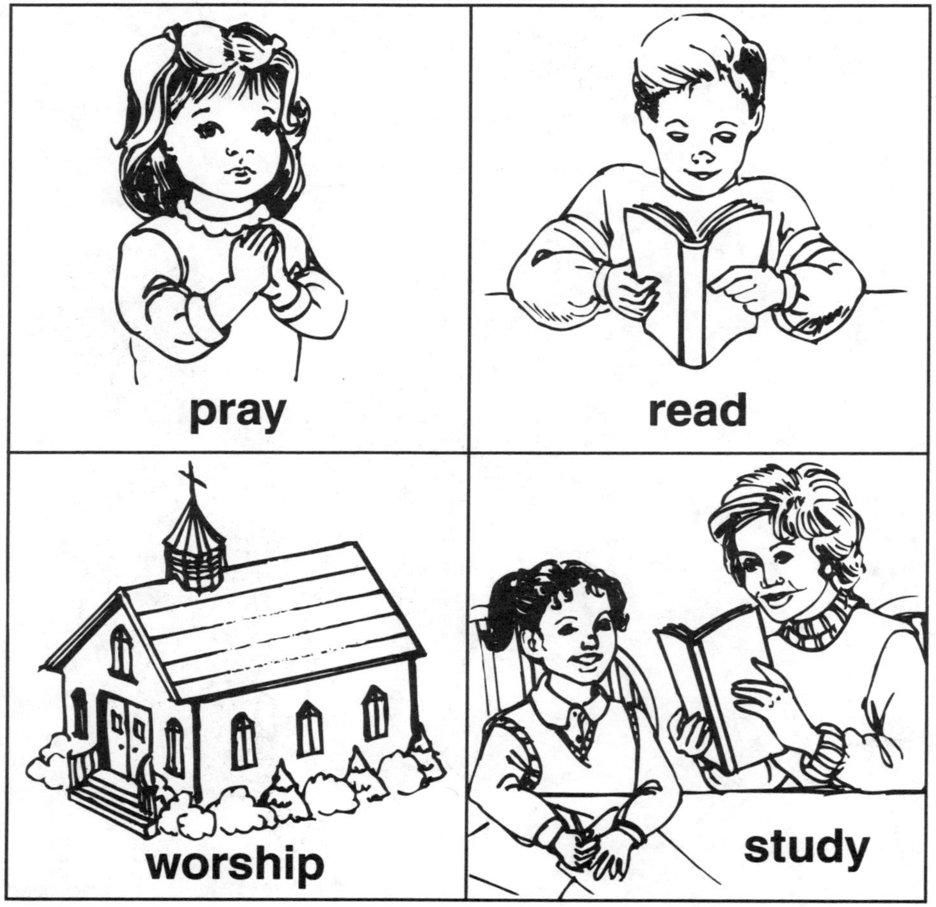

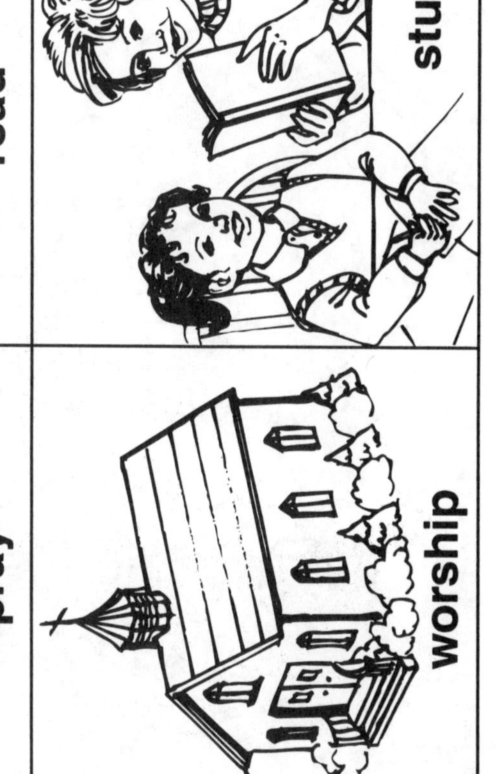

The Lord gave Moses and his people food in the desert.
Trace the words in the puzzle.

M
BREAD
N
N
HEAVEN

Draw the people with Moses.

Moses parted the sea.

When Boaz heard of Ruth's kindness to Naomi, he showed Ruth kindness in return.

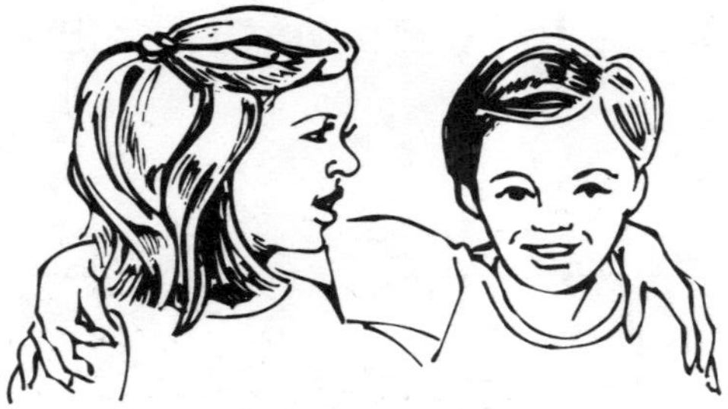

Draw something kind that someone did for you.

Draw something kind that you did for someone else.

Ruth

Color the picture of Ruth in the fields.

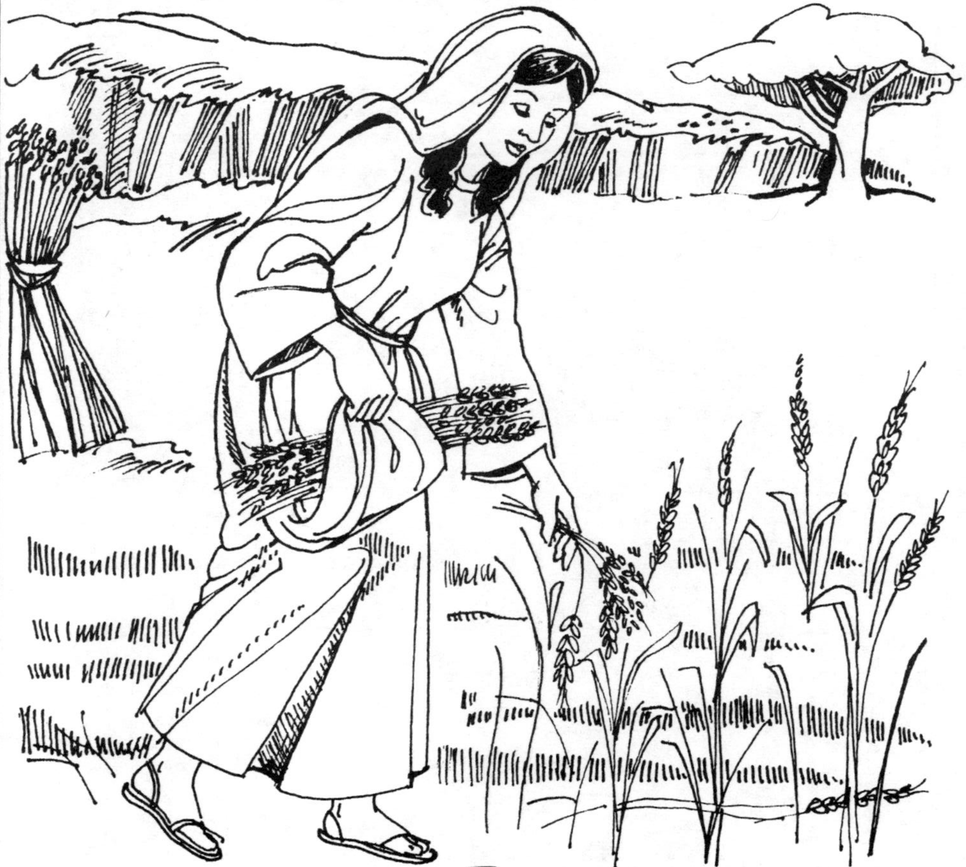

"Where you go I will go,
and where you stay I will stay."
Ruth 1:16

Ruth went back to Bethlehem
with Naomi.
Follow their path.

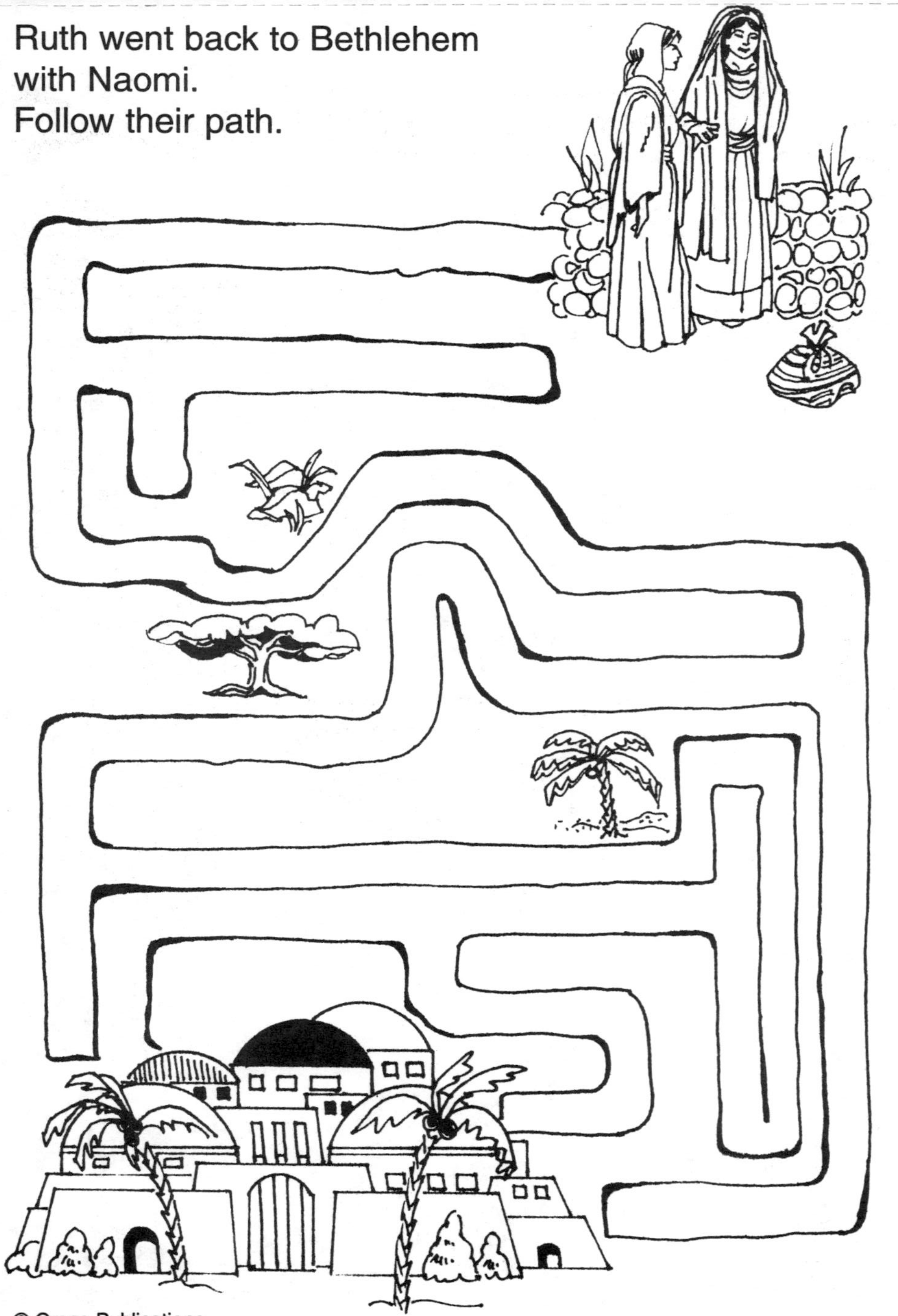

Find out what the name *Ruth* means.
Trace the lines and write the letters where they belong.

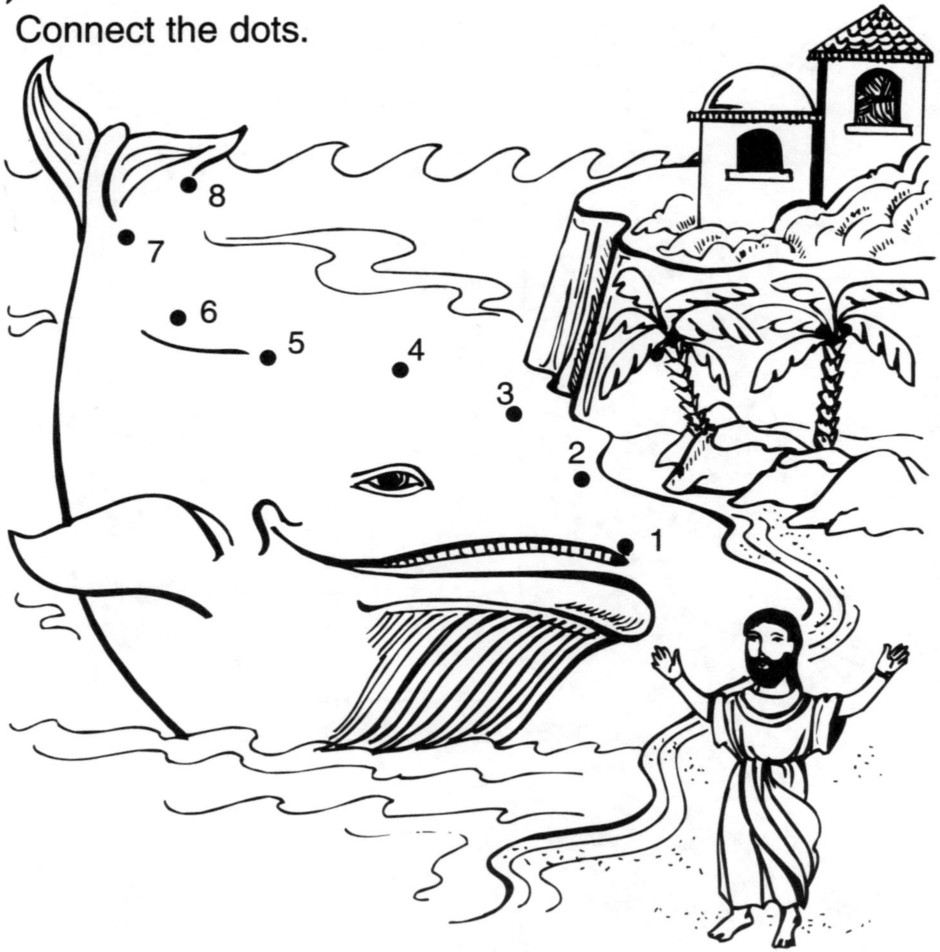

Draw your face.
Trace the heart.

I listen to God with my heart.

Jonah and the Big Fish

Connect the dots.

"In my distress I called to the Lord,
and he answered me."
Jonah 2:2

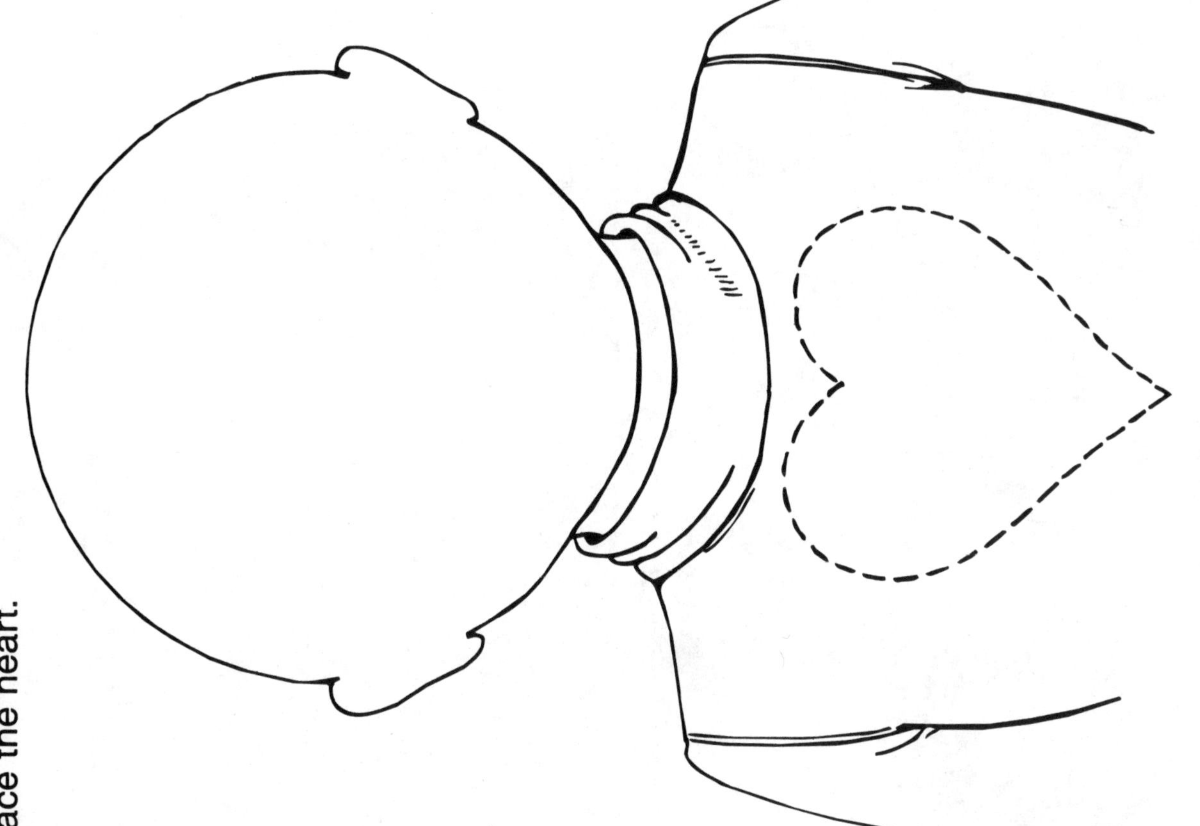

Jonah was in the belly of the fish for three days and three nights. Trace the numbers.

Jonah learned that God loves all people. Color the people.

Draw a picture of yourself singing.

Sing a song of praise.

Color Mary and the angel.

And Mary said: "My soul glorifies the Lord and my spirit rejoices in God my Savior…"
Luke 1:46-47

Mary hurried to tell her cousin Elizabeth
the news about her baby.
Trace Mary's path.

Mary praised God with her song.
Color the things that make music.

Jesus went with his family to Jerusalem.
Draw a picture of your family.

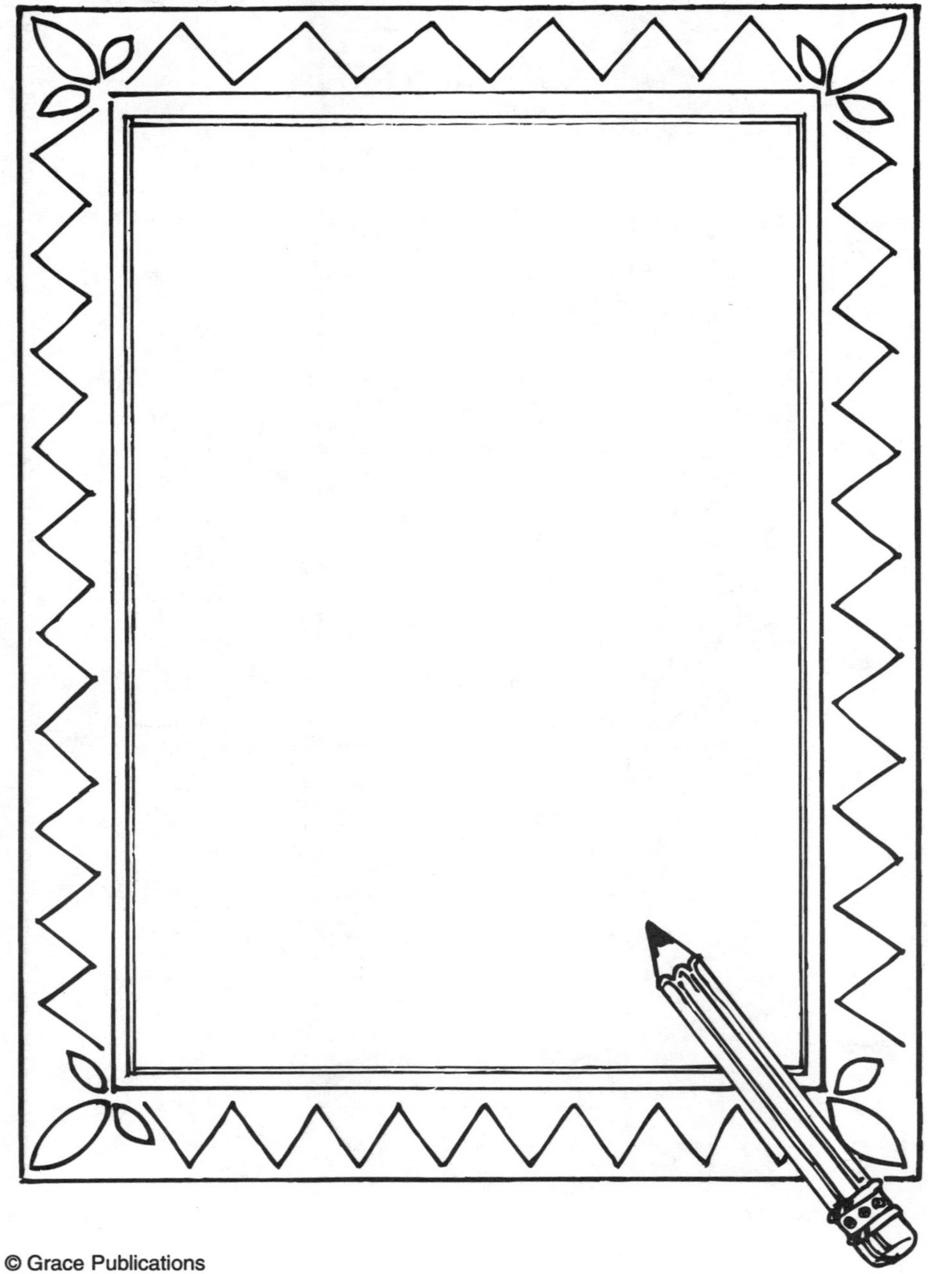

Jesus as a Boy

When Jesus was 12 years old, he went with his family to the temple in Jerusalem.
Connect the dots.

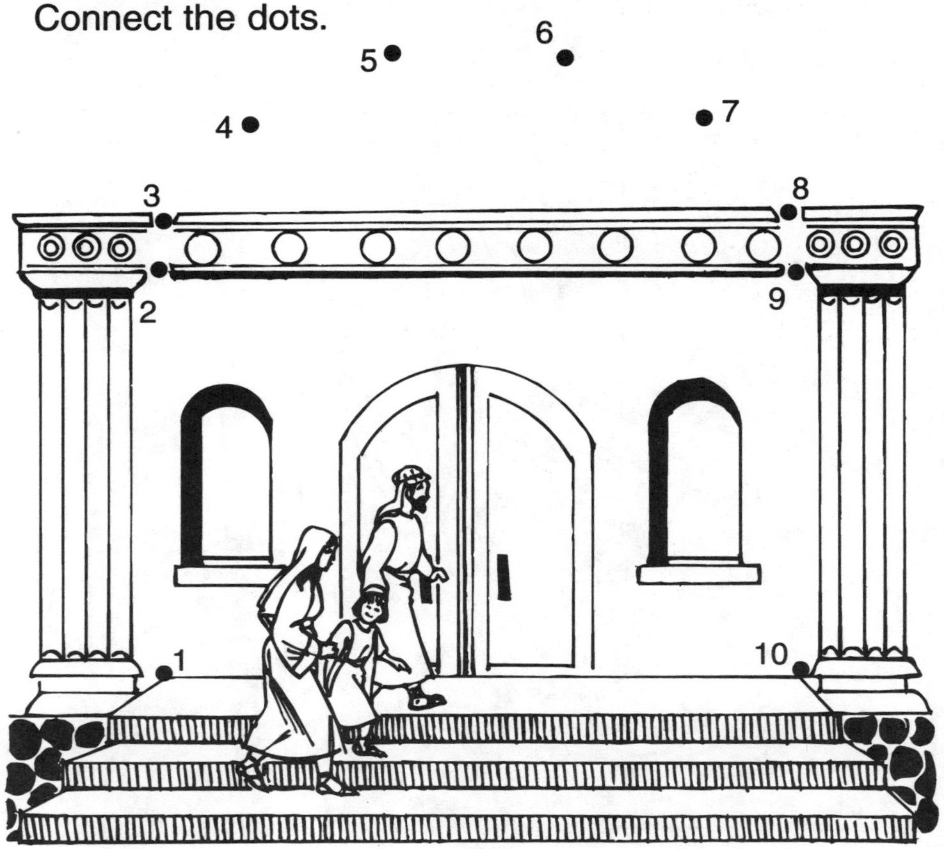

Then he went down to Nazareth with them
and was obedient to them.
Luke 2:51

Mary and Joseph couldn't find Jesus.
He was listening and asking questions in the temple.
Find Jesus in the picture. Color him.

The Bible tells us Jesus grew in wisdom.
Choose a word. Write it in the sentence.

I grow in ___________________.

Match the pictures that go together.
Draw a line.

Water for Life

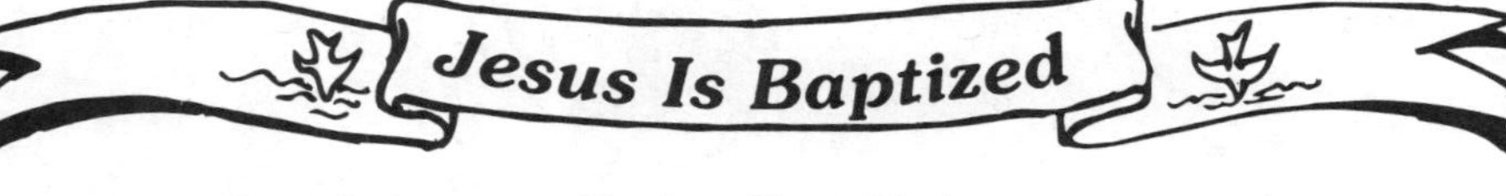

John baptized Jesus. Color the picture.

Trace the letters.

YOU ARE MY SON, WHOM I LOVE.

Find the name of the river where Jesus was baptized.
Trace the lines and write the letters where they belong.

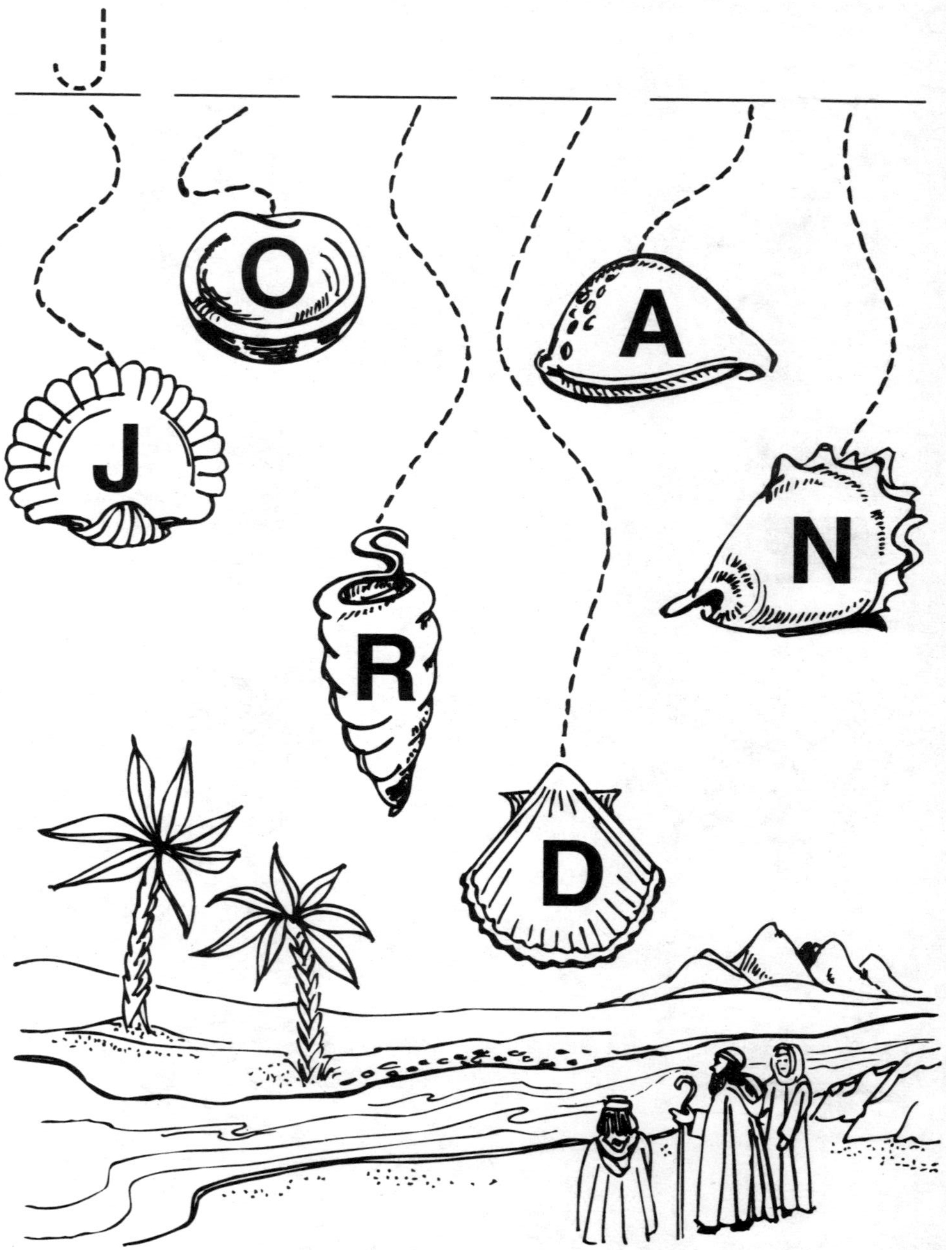

J _ _ _ _ _ _

God's Love for Me Overflows

Count and trace.

After Jesus fed the people, _____ baskets were left over.

The Loaves and the Fishes

Jesus spoke to five thousand people.
Color the picture.

"... and looking up to heaven, he gave thanks ..."
Mark 6:41

Jesus fed everyone with bread and fish.
Color the pictures.
Trace the words.

five

two

Find the words from the story.
Circle them.
Color the boxes with x.

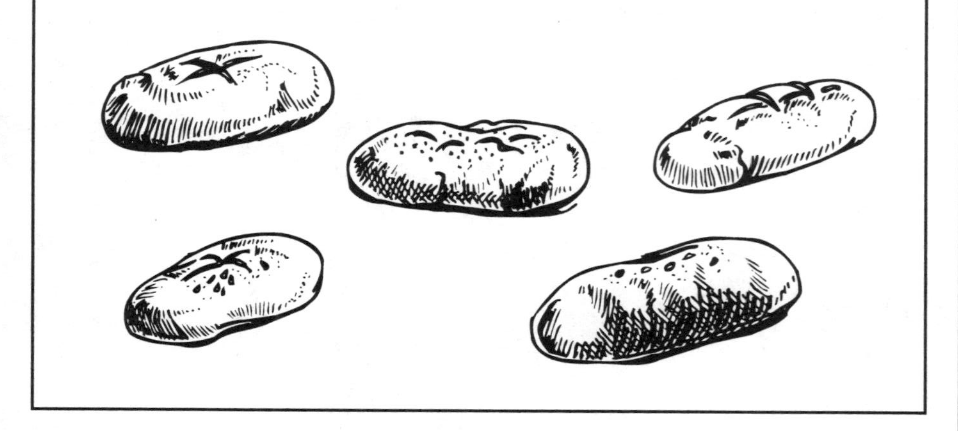

bread

Jesus

fish

feed

baskets

thanks

x	b	r	e	a	d	x
x	J	e	s	u	s	x
t	h	a	n	k	s	x
x	x	x	f	i	s	h
x	f	e	e	d	x	x
b	a	s	k	e	t	s

Mary and Joseph went to Bethlehem.
Follow their path.
Trace the words of the angel.
"I bring you good news of great joy."

The Birth of Jesus

Connect the dots.

"Glory to God in the highest . . ."
Luke 2:14

Match the pictures. Draw a line.

We celebrate the birth of Jesus.

WRITING PAPER

Draw a picture of yourself and a person sitting by you.

Neighbors

The Good Samaritan

The Samaritan helped the man on his way to Jericho.
Trace the picture.

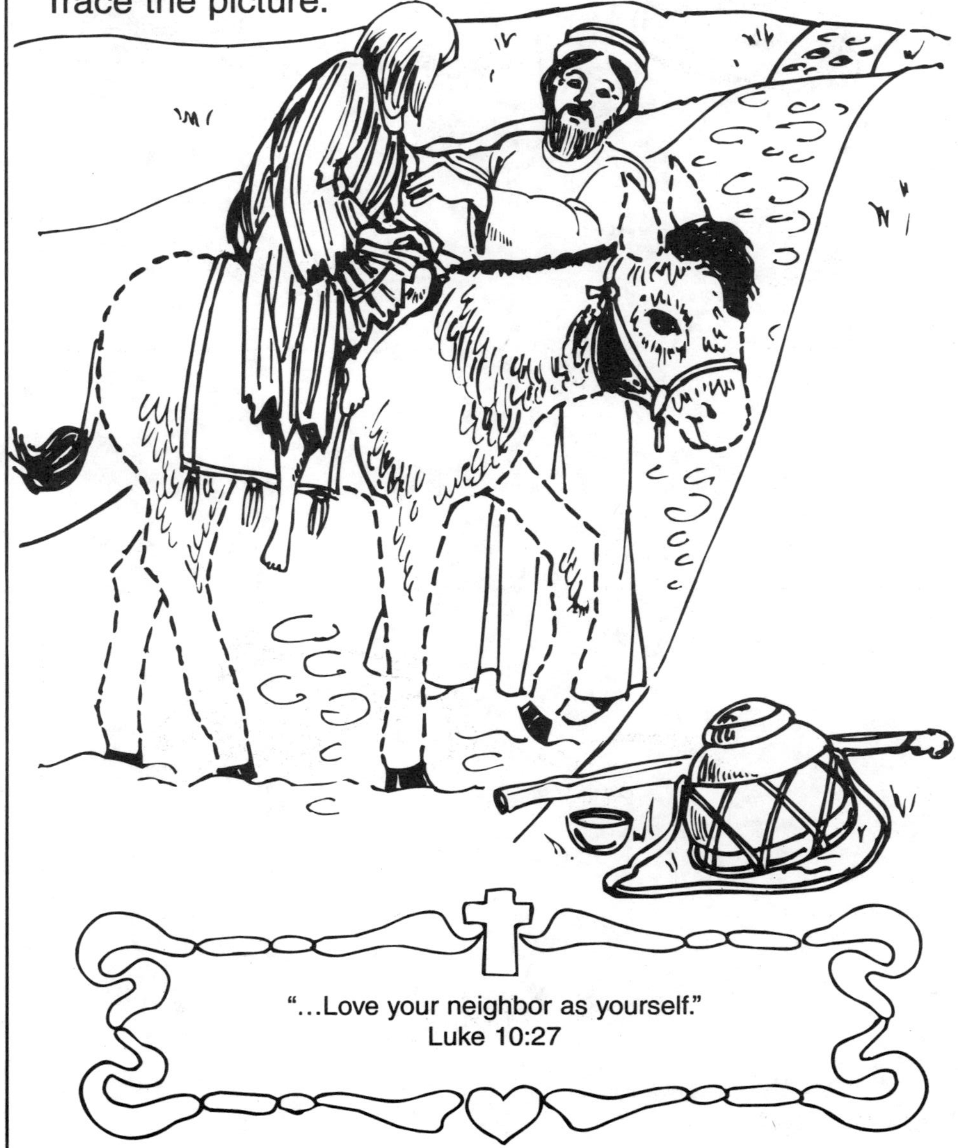

"...Love your neighbor as yourself."
Luke 10:27

Trace the hands.

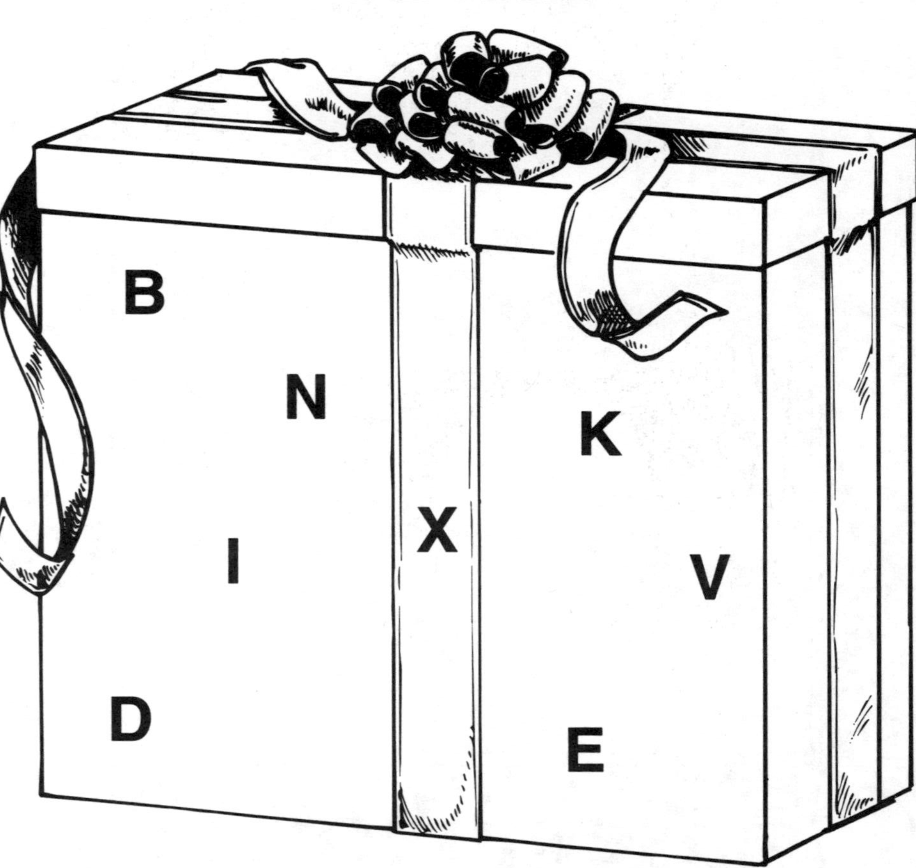

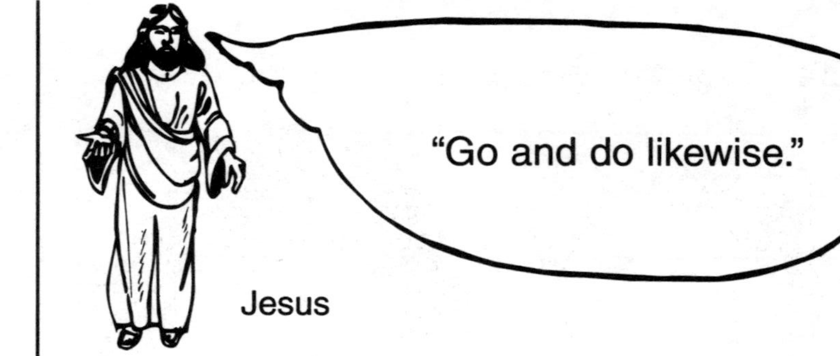

Find the letters and circle them.

BE KIND

The Lord's Prayer

Jesus teaches us to pray. Color the picture of Jesus.

...for your Father knows what you need before you ask him.
Matthew 6:8

Draw the faces of the children.

We pray the Lord's Prayer.

Trace the letters.

S E V I G R O F

G O D

Jesus told his friends to store up their treasures in heaven.
Trace the hearts.

Color the pictures.

Easter is a time of new life.

He Is Risen!

The women went to Jesus' tomb but he was gone. Trace their path.

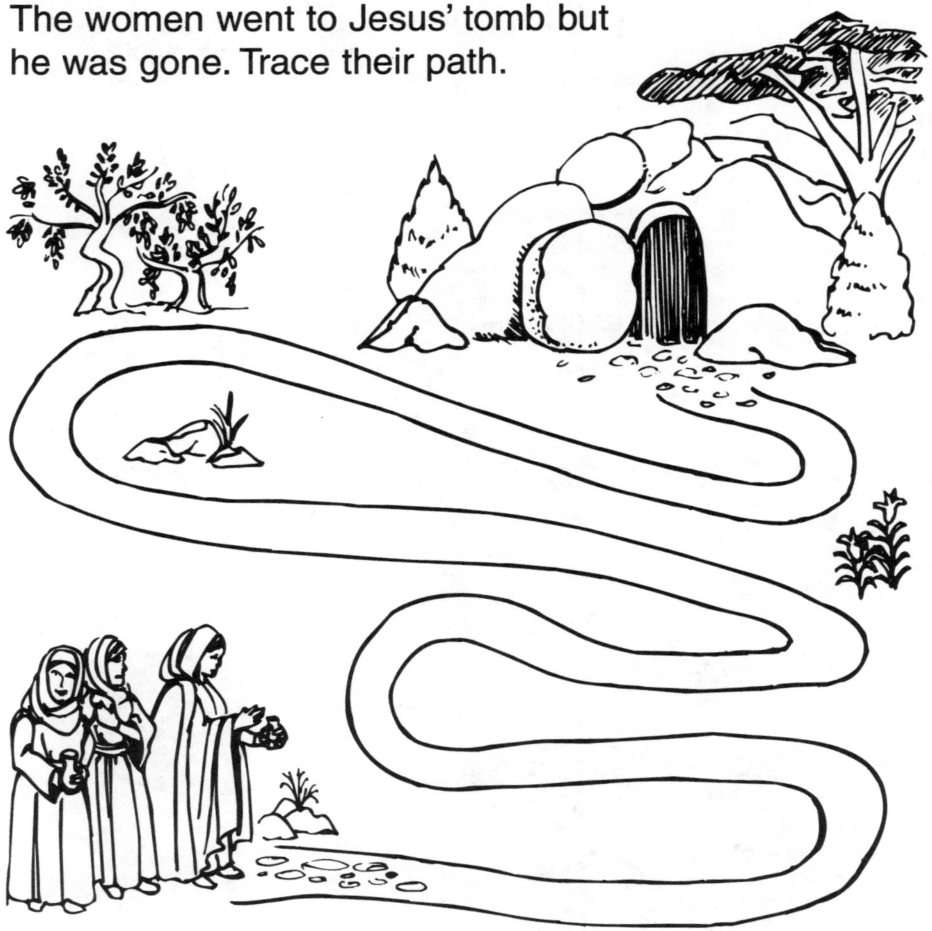

"Peace be with you! As the Father has sent me, I am sending you."
John 20:21

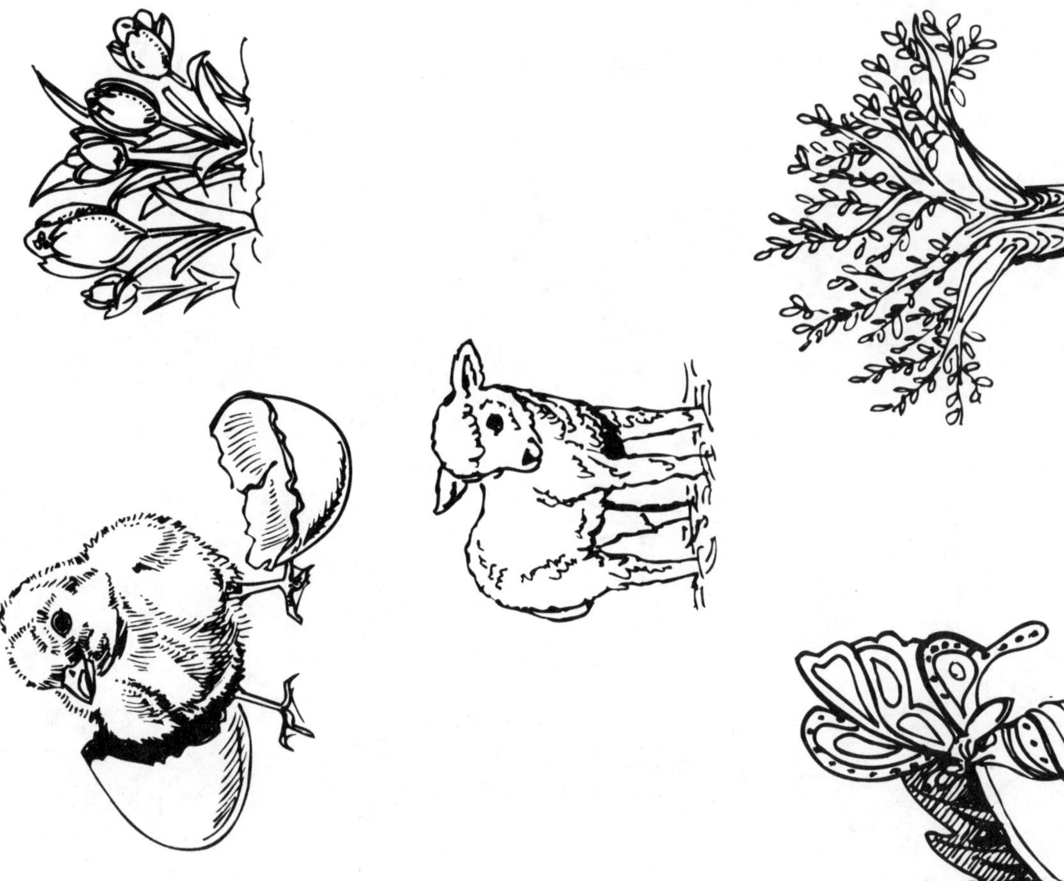

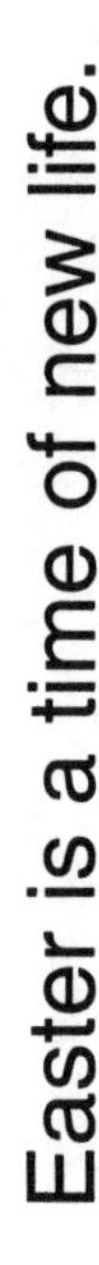

Trace the words of the angel at the tomb.

Trace the lines. Color the picture.